# THE CITY WAS ON FIRE AND WAS BEEN FOR WEEKS

## JAMES D QUINTON

a xplosive book

First published in 2010
Second edition published in 2012
by Xplosive Books

Copyright 2010 James D Quinton
Except* Copyright 2010 James D Quinton/Heidi James

The author's rights have been asserted in accordance
with the Copyright, Designs and Patents Act 1988

All rights reserved. No part of this publication may be
reproduced, stored in a retrieval system, or transmitted
in any form or by any means, electronic, mechanical,
photocopying, recording or otherwise, without the prior
written permission of the publisher, nor be otherwise
circulated in any form of binding or cover other than
that in which it is published and without a similar
condition including this condition being imposed
on the subsequent publisher

A CIP catalogue record for this book is available from
the British library

ISBN 978-0-9567823-1-1

"Don't think. Thinking is the enemy of creativity. It's self-conscious, and anything self-conscious is lousy. You can't try to do things. You simply must do things."

- Ray Bradbury

**Contents**

introduction, 1
she moulds my heart into an ashtray, 2
london (an announcement), 3
it will be morning, 4
flames, 5
bite, 6
Jenny, 8
dawn leaves us strangers, 11
dog, 12
'87, sunday morning/lunchtime, 13
boots crush sandy soil, 14
one night stand, 15
last kiss, 16
silver apricot, 17
the next big thing, 18
better than this, 19
Fragments of a Day, 20
streets of Holland, 22
your cock isn't special, 23
i can't see the night's sky for the light pollution below, 24
a little piece of anarchy, 25
on the shore, 27
oh, to be a captain of a starship, 28
The Last Time, 29
applying yourself, 32
workers of the world unite, 33
harvest moon, 34
sweetness of you, 35
I need a playwright to help me get my act together, 36
in eternity, 37
butchered sleep, 38
for her, 39
The Euthanasiaist, 40
ladies and gentlemen, from Los Angles, California, the Doors!, 47
the poets, 48

the street awakens, 49
maudlin winter, 50
check the amount and sign at the bottom, 51
strolling through London in the rain, 52
coma nation, 53
no one knows who I am or what I do, 54
england, 55
the sky exploded, 56
The Supermarket Dissolved As The Past Echoed Through To The Present (with Heidi James), 57
the jam, 63
contorted with passion, 64
I don't want to lose you before love has begun, 65
unannounced, 66
Cadence, 67
stallone, 70
sanctuary in a magritte, 71
sympathetic, but swift, 72
new york (an announcement), 73
your secrets, 74
and she knows it, 75
the comeback, 76
The Writer, 77
golden tanned flesh, 78
feel all famous five, 79

**2012 Second Edition Bonus Content**

baby, there's an app for that, 80
November Hotel, 81
after...., 92
schoolgirls look more like porn stars these days, 93
the girl with the jet black hair, 94
the last dance, 95
an immortal line, 96
and I snapped, 97
elsewhere, 98

**introduction**

flash communication!

they said it wouldn't happen!

how many times can I use the word 'some'?

some (1) very, very old poems, glimpses into the past, ghosts…
some (2) old short stories, some (3) poems that missed the *Street Psalms* boat, some (4) new poems….

a collection…

4, no, 5

the roads are veins and the heart almost stops

magic music in the heart of desolation

moving slowly in sepia

**she moulds my heart into an ashtray**

sweet hot woman
elusive, fey
draws me into
her danger
her spark
her fire
ignites us

high heels
blood red lipstick
shortest of floral
dresses
her walk
strong
determined
doesn't   give   a   damn

my heart is hers
she takes it
into her furnace
melts
reshapes
cools hard
moulded into
an ashtray
where she deposits
the cinders
of her cigarette
a cloud of smoke
blows through
those full lips
and I'm just
a memory


(2010)

**london (an announcement)**

flash communication!
the city is asleep
crime is in the capital
and is escalating to the beat!
dusk soon turns to darkness
and the street lights flicker on
the rain hits the pavement
but where have all the people gone?

sirens break the silence
and the criminals take one last gasp
but all is forgotten
as the businessman walks past


*(1996)*

**it will be morning**


the light that wouldn't come
rises, unwilling, at first,
it lingers, just a haze

but do you remember the
preceding hours
when we talked so much
we ran out of words
and there wasn't
anything more
I could tell you
and there wasn't
anything more
you could tell me

so we sat, drank,
exchanged glances
and knowing smiles

and now exhausted
I ask if I can sleep
on your couch

you tell me there is
fresh coffee for later

and go to bed

leaving me to
imagine that you
placed a kiss
on my cheek


*(2009)*

**flames**

hypnotic
wisps of
orange
dance in
the air

slivers
of
heat rising
on the
wind

hands
held out

the dark
of the night
dissolves

my eyes
transfixed

my thoughts
wander

as I
watch

the
flames

*(2005)*

**bite**

seized
by a
fevered
grip

your body
dragged
with heels
kicking
across a
dusty
floor

light
diminishes
as a
dark
arid
environment
prevails

hands tied
behind back
to a
rickety
wooden
chair

cold
sweat
tr
ic
kl
ing

temptation
rises within
as in front
of you
*that* sin
*your* sin
the one
that gets
you
every time

the one
you can't
shake off

winking
licking
its lips
giving an
over
friendly wave

it waits
for you
to lean
forward and

bite


(2009)

# Jenny

A few weeks ago I lost my job, my woman left, and then my dog got run over by a car that was driven by a guy with a bad Sinatra cut. I didn't think things could get any worse until I met Jenny. It was late. I was sitting in a downtown bar nursing my seventh beer, taking a pull on a Marlboro, when this woman with a cheap dye job sat herself down next to me.

'Hiya hun, I'm drinking vodka and coke, are you buying?'

I looked her up and down. Apart from the barkeep she was the only person who'd spoken to me in weeks. She was wearing a low cut top; her breasts pushed up in danger of spilling out, a mini and high heels, all clashing primary colours. She was about forty, but was trying to look twenty. Her skin resembled a something you might pull from a fried chicken bucket.

I gestured to the barkeep. 'Paul, get the lady a vodka and coke.'

'*Lady?*'

'Make it a double, Paul. My name's Jenny, what's yours?'

'Richard, Rick, whatever.'

'Like Richard Gere?'

'Yeah, honey, and you are my pretty woman.'

The barkeep put the double vodka down in front of Jenny.

'Have you got a spare ciggie, hun?' I passed her one. 'Thanks. So whatcha doin' here?'

'A few drinks, I've had a rough time.'

'Ain't we all?' She blew out a cloud of smoke. 'How about I make things good for you again?'

'I don't know, I'm still getting over someone.'

'What are you? A faggot?'

'No.' I washed down the remains of the beer and indicating for another.

'Okay, so oral is twenty, straight sex is fifty.'

Paul put the new beer down in front of me. Once again I looked her up and down, it had been a while, too long. 'Okay, how about I give one hundred to spend the night?'

'*One hundred?*' Her shriek made the rest of the drinkers turn round and stare. 'Sure hun, you got a deal!'

Jenny downed the rest of her drink. I threw a twenty onto the bar and we left.

'It's this way.' I said when we got outside.

'Wait a minute, hun. I gotta get my stuff.'

'Stuff?'

'Yeah, my landlord threw me out. Said I was a whore, can you believe that?'

'Right….' I ran my hand over my stubble, regretting my decision.

Jenny disappeared down a side alley and reappeared dragging a suitcase on coasters behind her.

As we walked to my place she started telling me about her car crash of a life. '…and then I had another abortion….'

'Terrible….' I muttered, as we reached the door of to my house.

We went in.

Jenny dumped her stuff and then walked up to me and grabbed my groin. 'So, you want it in here or upstairs?'

'Err… how about some food? I'm hungry.'

'Hey, I can cook….'

'Urm….'

It was too late Jenny trotted into the kitchen. I sat down and sighed. She came out with a beer. 'Here you go, hun.'

I took the beer. I needed it. Taking a hit, I pulled out my wallet and counted out the hundred. She giggled, stuffed in her bra and returned the kitchen.

After about fifteen minutes Jenny came back into the living room and opened her suitcase.

'What are you doing?'

'Time to give you your moneys worth, hun.' She pulled out two pairs of handcuffs.

'Oh, I don't think so.'

'Come on upstairs.'

In the bedroom Jenny went to work. She stripped me down to my bare ass, handcuffed my hands behind my back and pushed me onto the bed. She then handcuffed my legs together and went to work.

'How does it feel, hun?' She was chewing bubblegum.

It did feel good.

After a few minutes I smelt burning. Jenny looked up and sniffed. 'Oh no, the food!'

She got up and rushed downstairs.

I could hear her screaming. I tried to get up but couldn't get far. I started shouting at her to come and uncuff me.

But she didn't return. Smoke started to rise and it soon filled the property. I managed to get up and shuffle to the window, I undone the latch and worked my way out. I fell fifteen feet to the ground; my ex-wife's shrubbery broke my fall. Flames were licking out of the house and my neighbours were all in the street watching. I got myself up right and hopped away from the burning building with my cock and balls bouncing up and down in full view of everybody.

As I watched the house burn, I turned to see Jenny, half way down the road, dragging her suitcase behind her, fixing her knickers.

*(2003)*

**dawn leaves us strangers**

burning together
under
artificial lighting
where
savage love
has reduced
us without speech

the dirty mattress
fits our
crime

the dark night
with its
howls
and
screams
is all
we have
left to cling
to

dawn leaves
us
strangers


*(2009)*

**dog**

the dog
next door
barks
crazy
loud yelps

dancing in circles
on his hind legs
seemingly driven
wild
by the vibrations
of the wind

it must be that
because
there is
nothing
else there

*(2004)*

**'87, sunday morning/lunchtime**

social club
small coke
lukewarm on lips
cheese and onion crisps
smoking at the bar
fruit machines
bowling green,
immaculate,
space invaders
fire doors slamming shut


*(2010)*

**boots crush sandy soil**


white smoke in the distance
rises against a sharp blue sky
the weather, for once, as
the meteorologists predicted

my boots crush sandy soil and gravel
sweat pours from my brow
rabbits dash to their burrows
small birds flit from tree to tree

and above

92 million miles away
the scorching sun

at its centre
hydrogen nuclei
fuses into helium

yellow, gold
orange, red
white hot

burning


*(2009)*

**one night stand**


in a crowded bar
our eyes met
no words, just passion

that night, juxtaposed, naked
99, 69, 99,
sweating, moving as one
reaching for heaven

in the morning, two
people, who just
hours ago had been
so close, now
a million miles apart


*(2004)*

**last kiss**

by candlelight
that flickers from a draft
coming through a
Georgian window
from which
the moon shines through
we share

one

last kiss

and in that brief moment
I recall our sensual encounters
where our hands danced across
our bodies and we created our
own heaven

*(2009)*

**silver apricot**

beautiful enchanting tree
fan shaped leaves
soft delicate yellow flowers

*(2000)*

**the next big thing**

on the way to
the park to feed
the ducks
on a sunny
autumnal afternoon
waking through
mountains
of golden leaves
we passed four
guys sitting on a
knee high wall
dressed in Oxfam
bearded, hair long,
one holding a beaten
acoustic guitar

'they look like
like the next big thing,'
my girlfriend whispered

'they probably
sound like the last
big thing,'
I replied

we continued by
as the one
holding the guitar
started to strum
a tired melody

*(2003)*

**better than this**


throwing up
after a heavy night out

head hung over toilet
the bathroom spins

I remember
the drinks
the dancing
the woman
the kebab
the long walk home
well, long stumble home

now I strain
and choke
nose running
eyes watering
fingers clenched
gut wrenching

my only hope is
to shrink and disappear
between the holes
in the bathroom lino
because it has got
to be better than this


(2005)

# Fragments of a Day

*"One must still have chaos in oneself to be able to give birth to a dancing star"*
- Friedrich Nietzsche

Naked at last, free from the clothing that had been suffocating me all day. I lie on my bed, spreading myself out. I am grateful because for a hot sunny day it's thankfully cool in my bedroom. The sun is going down. My eyelids close watching the shadow of the sun diminishing on the wall.

\*

I awake at sometime between three and four in the morning. I sit up and rub my face, my neck is stiff and I feel at little out of it. I get up and take a piss, then make a cup of tea. With my tea in hand I walk into the living room and flick on the TV, always the best time of day to watch TV, the early hours of the day. There is some non-descript American chat show on. I sigh and watch, not listening, but just watching. A spider crawls across the floorboards. He stops. He sits in between the TV and me. Staring.

\*

I'm standing against the bar in my favourite pub. A girl walks in wearing a tee that says, 'Tonight, I'm Single'. She approaches the bar and orders a rum and coke.
    "Hi," I say.
    "Hi," she tentatively replies, brushing back her blonde hair.
    "I see we've got something in common."
    "We have?" A smile worked its way across her face. I stare at her chest. "Oh right."
    The barman hands her the drink. I pull out a five note and pay.

\*

In the storeroom I reach up and pull down an outer of Mayfair cigarettes. My boss nods at me as he walks through. He's going to get another four pack of beer. Or perhaps two four packs of beer. He's drinking more and more. He looks terrible. Four days unshaven, four days in the same clothes. I walk back through to the shop and watch him struggling with the cans. A customer approaches the counter. I glance at the clock: 2pm. I've been here since 5am. Only three hours to go.

"Yes mate, how can I help?"

\*

I awake. It's dark outside. I check the time. 9pm. Two more hours before the pub closes. I get up, wash, and change my clothes. I stick a frozen meal in the microwave and set it to incinerate. It takes three minutes to cook. Four minutes to eat. Five minutes after that I'm walking to the pub.

\*

"I like your eyes," comments the blonde as we lie on her bed. "They're not blue or green, grey perhaps."

"Well, it says blue on my birth certificate."
"No, they're grey."
"Ok. What time is it?"
"Three am."
"God, I need some sleep."
"Hey, I'm not finished with you yet!"

*(2003)*

**the streets of Holland**


a fine taste
'white witch',
numero one

straight from the
streets of Holland
to my front room
in England

mixed with
golden tobacco
and lovingly rolled
with a flick of my wrist
a flame ignites

as the end burns     I inhale deep

a smooth rush of
smoke hits my lungs
altering perception
and after a while time

my body lies limp
as I float over a
soundtrack of jazz

but my mind
touching all realities
transcending all possibilities

aware of everything
but caring about nothing


*(2004)*

**your cock isn't special**

I read
your derivative
sexist shit
in
horror
yes, Bukowski
was great
and Miller was
a
mischievous
bastard
but it's
all been
said now

your
cock isn't
special

and what
you imagine
you do with
it isn't
interesting


*(2008)*

**I can't see the night's sky for the light pollution below**


I didn't believe her
when she said:
"there are no stars in London"
but there aren't

there is only an
orange yellow haze
light trapped
giving a sense
of a city that never sleeps

I never would have imagined
not being able to look up and
see one of hundreds, thousands
of bright shinning dots
framed against an expanse of black

and the moon, of course
I have stood in a field at midnight
cigarette in hand
looking up at a full harvest moon
in awe and wonder

but here in London
on a wet winter night
I can't see the night's sky
for the light pollution below


(2005)

**a little piece of anarchy**

we must have
stood
out a

mile

wearing
long trench
coats
in
the heart
and heat
of summer

we had
a gift
stealing

we always
went for
porn mags
batteries
posters
books
cds
sweets

it was all
about
the
bu
z
z

that rush

of
adrenalin

fear
and
excitement

combined

more
powerful

then
any
drug


*(2006)*

**on the shore**

fine lines
paint and picture
I stand and wait
for the tide

a cold wind
cuts through warm clothes

the body shivers
muscles become tense

softer than shadows
remaining calm
when we catch
each other's eyes


(2001)

**oh, to be a captain of a starship**

Captain *J.T Kirk*
now there *was*
a man who
*always* got a piece

Captain…
the girls always
like a Captain

i think of that
moment when he was
up to his neck
in tribbles

but usually
that guy was
up to his neck
in pussy

(2005)

# The Last Time

I dipped a toe into the water; the temperature was just right. I slid off my silk Japanese bathrobe and stepped into the tub and lowered my body into the white bubble covered aqua. As I descended, the water flooded in around me, the sensation of the liquid warmth covering my skin. I flicked my hair behind me and tipped my head back and sighed. As I lay there, the smell of green grass incense wafted through from the living room. I had meant to put a stick or two on in here, in the bathroom, to help me unwind, but the gentle fragrance drifting in was pungent enough for it to work its magic. Breaking the water's surface with my right foot, I perched it on the inside edge of the bath, the sudden hotness of the skin blending with the cold ambience of the air, producing a cool relaxing sensation.

As she drifted into an abated sleep, she suddenly remembered something, a thought, which caused her to abruptly sit up. Upon rising, with such necessity, a sharp inundation of H2O decanted from her previously submerged frame, and now, as she sat vertical, her mind unsettled, beads of water cascaded along her skin, pulled by gravity, outlining her exposed body, causing her to shiver.

I cupped a handful of water and splashed it over my face, as if to give myself a wake up call, letting my conscience, my mind know not to forget such things, although it had been a long day, a tiring day. As soon as I got in all I wanted was a bite to eat, a bath and then bed. But this one-dimensional frame of mind had pushed aside affairs that should not have been sidelined. I reluctantly rose from my capacious Victorian bathtub and stepped out on to the cold wooden floorboards. The excess water rode down me towards the floor, soaking the area around my feet, as the air drew breaths on my skin. I unfolded a large, fluffy cream towel and began to dry myself, at first slowly, with long pleasurable swabs, my hand in the cotton breaching my waterlogged pubic hairs, but then as my mind calculated events and timing I rubbed with more vigour until I felt dry enough to dress.

She wrapped herself back into her elegantly decorated robe and trotted on tiptoes through her open plan flat to her bedroom. Flinging off her robe she pulled herself into a pair of jeans that had lain crumbled in a heap at the end of her bed. She caught her reflection in the window, her breasts firm, and her stomach flat. From the window of her flat she had the perfect view of the city skyline. She gazed out, once again seemingly separated from her previous endeavours, staring longingly over the panorama. She could see a city, a city that never slept, forever lost in perpetual capitalist motion. Lights emanated from other flats adjacent to hers; she could see the occupants sitting, walking, and relaxing in the comfort of their homes and the material comfort of their possessions. She wondered if they could see her, standing almost aloof, top half bare. She backed away from the window and drew the blinds.

I snapped back to reality and hurriedly searched my wardrobe for a top, anything, something causal. Finding a black long sleeved t-shirt I pulled it over my skin, it hugged the dampness of my flesh, clinging to me like a scared child. With myself dressed, I headed for the hallway and checked my reflection in the oval ornate gold beaded mirror. I looked far from my best, my hair hung tangled and unkempt, my face makeup-less, showing my age, a frivolous and debauched few years had finally caught up with me. I slipped on a pair on trainers, picked up my car keys and left the warmth of my flat. I was going to be late, but then again I was always late, always fashionably late.

She took the elevator to the walled in, security guarded ground floor car park. Outside, amongst the moulded metal and rubber she found herself gazing up at the night sky. The stars and the moon are the only thing I can rely on, she thought as they shone down, the only thing in my life that has always been constant. As she found her way to her car she thought back to when it had all begun; a creeping, knowing smile worked its way across her face.

I drove out of the luminous city, past blocks of flats similar to my own, past out of town shopping centres, past boarded up council houses and brownfield industrial wastelands left vacant, as nature reclaimed what was once hers. My mind, once again, started separating itself from the here and now, my thoughts up there in the heavens. I ached for my bed after such an exacting day; this was the last thing I needed, but I'm a woman of my word, I have to be, I have to retain some sense of self as I've lost so much else.

As she drove her car stereo was playing an album by the Doors, the music sedative and seductive washing over her, blending with inattentive cogitations. As the track L.A. Women reverberated around her car she tapped her long-finger nailed digits on the steering wheel. The cars that passed on the narrow, winding road, their head lights dipped for the darkness, danced in front of her pale blue eyes.

It didn't take long to reach the forest, its dense wooded façade merging with, and then encompassing, the agricultural landscape that had preceded it. I knew this journey all to well, the drive here once filling me with a carnal excitement. Soon, hidden by the night, a dirt track, which last time had begun to overgrow in the humid, wet springtime climate with ferns, nettles and bramble, would become accessible.

She turned off the asphalt road on to the gravel path, the tyres of the car crushing and casting up dust and soil into the air. As she drove deeper and deeper into the forest, the trees became thicker and thicker, blocking out any natural light that was gifted by the moon and the stars. Turning from the straight track, her car entered a small clearing where ahead a dim light illuminated the inside of a solitary parked car. She parked a few metres away from the other vehicle, avoiding eye contact with its driver.

It had started as something fun, something divergent, something, which was uniquely ours. It had taken me from an embittered affinity with a man I'd known since childhood to the edges of a liberated contentment. But now, like everything that went before it, it had become repetitive, the edge, the agitation and most significantly, the pleasure had gone. It had all been replaced by an empty dull feeling, a lead weight of ritual that was now beginning to tear me away from the fresh path that I was walking, a path that I'd desired for a long time. This, I now decided, had to be, would be, the last time.

*(2006)*

**applying yourself**

one of the most
depressing things ever
filling out multiple
applications forms
writing and then re-writing
the same information
over and over
being reminded
of all the terrible jobs
making me miserable
I also realise that my efforts
will probably be in vain
as I have no enthusiasm
all I manage to do is repeat
the same tired and tested lies

deep sighs come fast
and for a moment
I want to throw my hands
in the air admit defeat
and go join the bums
in the leafy park
drinking super strength cider
and laughing about nothing
as our teeth slowly rot

*(2004)*

**workers of the world unite**

the revolution
will not
be
televised
but will
probably,
at some point,
end up on
you tube

*(2009)*

**harvest moon**

wide
white
yellow
lonesome moon
radiates
on a dark
winter sky
canvass

surface visible
dark patches
a collage
of mystery
indentations
shadows

I stand
I watch
my hands dug
deep into pockets

it passes slowly
through the heavens

*(2010)*

**the sweetness of you**

let us embrace
under the golden
midnight moon
so close
so immense
we can see craters
and imprints

the sweetness of you

the starry sky


*(2009)*

**I need a playwright to help me get my act together**


it's on my mind
continuously

constant
like a flowing river
or an alcoholics thirst

every minute that passes
the thought of
soft flesh

curves
breasts
lips
thighs
and
legs

tempt me

everyday brings the
same impulses

and everyday
I try to resist

but I need a playwright
to help me get my act together


*(2005)*

**in eternity**

it's late
we're lying
on your bed
and through the window
we can see
stars flecked across
the blue black sky
a rich soundscape
flows, warm, beautiful
we're smothered in a joy
it belongs to us
it nourishes us
it taps into a spirit
somehow we
connect without touch
without speech or sight
we're lost somewhere
in eternity, together
the record crackles as
the needle follows
the grooves
and where we
are now is
so real
I hear you breathing
I see your
chest rise
and fall
then I feel
the heat of
your hand
on mine

*(2009)*

**butchered sleep**

petrified at dawn
sticky sweat
my sheets
twisted around me
my heart
beating
throbbing
to the whispers
in my head
haunting
words
dr
op
pi
ng
to my tongue
I cannot speak

I lie
awake
counting shadows
moving across
the wall

cars rumble
past my window

aside from them
it's quiet

*(2005)*

**for her**


we take a long walk
that follows a narrow gravel path
that leads along the coast
the relentless sea
crashes against
the rocks below
and a resolute wind blows
through your hair

it tangles

and my heart leaps
when your wide smile
and blue eyes
greet me

I hold your hand tighter

and we press on

some hours later
back in the rented cabin
I light the fire
put on a record
you pour the wine
then relax in my arms


(2009)

### The Euthanasiaist

I step off the plane. This country is new to me. Advertising material only gave me badly taken, digitally enhanced photographs and brief sentences that described what I would see. But I'm taken aback at the spectacular picturesque splendour. The mountains dominate the landscape into the horizon, expanding up towards the heavens, as snow lies blanketed all around. I seize a lungful of the air; it's cold and pure.

In the arrivals lounge I mingle with the tourists, many of them, as you'd expect, here for the skiing. I sit down. I'm tired. I watch families stride in excited at being on holiday. They struggle with their over-packed suitcases. I don't have any luggage to collect. My belongings for this journey are efficiently packed in my black leather briefcase, embossed with my initials. I always travel light.

The airport itself looks like science fiction novel vision of the future - steel and glass, clean, smooth lines. If my imagination allowed me, outside could be an alien world, maybe the moon. Thousands of people pass each other in anonymity. I feel a warm tingling sensation radiate through me. I like it here.

I order a cup of coffee in the restaurant and sit myself down in a brown leather armchair. I had intentionally caught an earlier plane to allow myself this opportunity to relax and enjoy the experience, to be able soak up some of the surroundings. Life these days is so rushed, so regimented, it seems like we're stuck in a perpetual time and motion study – if every second of the day is not crammed with a productive action, then you're a lazy so-and-so.

I lean over to the table next to mine and pick up a copy of an English broadsheet. I open it up and start to read it from back to front. I always read a newspaper that way. The monotonous stuff is at the back, the sport, the advice and lonely-hearts columns and the obituaries. Actually, I like obituaries. Ten minutes pass and I finally give into temptation. I pull out a packet of cigarettes; I slide one out and put it between my lips. I dig deep into my pockets and find the pack of matches that I took from the London hotel I stayed in last night. I only allow myself one cigarette a day otherwise I simply wouldn't be able to cope with the repugnant smell. The burnt tobacco and chemicals hit my lungs just as I notice a 'No Smoking' sign.

I feel I must tell you a bit about myself. Okay, so without sounding like I've joined AA or something: my name's Peter Wyreham, I'm fifty-five years old, up until very recently I worked as an investment banker in London - made quite a lot of money - I have brown eyes and thinning brown hair. I'm single and have been for some time now. I'm also dying - just thought I'd slip that in. I have cancer, terminal cancer. I'm in pain constantly. I've come here to die.

Do you remember that German guy who ate a man? What was his name now? Oh yes, Armin Meiwes. He had advertised on the internet for "well-built man, 18-30 years old, for slaughter.' Direct and to the point. I like that in an advertisement. He found a willing victim in Bernd Brandes. After amputating Brandes's penis, Meiwes fried it in salt, pepper and garlic and they both dined. Brandes was later killed and Meiwes gradually ate the body over several months. Apparently there was, or at least there might have been some kind of sexual motive for both men. As I think about that horror, an old joke comes back to me. Where I heard it I no longer remember. Maybe it was told to me by one of the younger guys at the office. It's about a Jewish woman (why she is Jewish escapes me, maybe the lilt of a Jewish pronunciation makes it funnier?). When asked why she was cooking her husband's manhood she replies; 'For forty years I've had to eat it his way, now he's going to eat it my way.' The corner of my mouth ascends and I choke back an adolescent giggle.

Emerging from the innovate building, I hail a cab to take me into the city. The exquisiteness of Switzerland again strikes me as the German-speaking driver ferries me into Zurich, weaving between the classical carved buildings and trams. The architecture is breathtaking. As someone who once designed his own home (second home actually, in Scotland) I feel I can ostentatiously enjoy it more than most. It's like being transported back a hundred or so years. Yet the contemporary structures like the airport and the shopping malls fit effortlessly with the past. Truly this may be, in terms of human colonisation, the most striking place on Earth. It's all so clean, the streets are free of litter, the pavements swept, leaves from the trees absent after falling, and the crystal refection of the river Limmat nearby, the whiteness of the snow and the crisp cool of the air help to add to the overall effect. Taking off my leather gloves, I reach into my black woollen overcoat, pull out a bottle of hand sanitizer and apply some of the liquid into my palms.

The cabdriver drops me off and I head for the nearest department store. As I purposefully packed so little, I need to buy a few items. In fact I've only brought a toothbrush, toothpaste, comb, nail clippers and nail file, one three bladed razor, a small tube of shaving foam, skin moisturiser, deodorant – unscented - and a polish-cloth for my shoes. All the items are separately sealed in polythene bags. Admittedly I'm not going to need much. My suit, shirt and tie are good for another day's wear – although I do feel a little anxious about that. But I don't want to spend my last day in dirty underwear, so a new vest, underpants and socks are a must, plus I'm also going to purchase a flannel, a bar of unscented soap and a small towel for my ablutions.

*My last day*. Peculiarly enough that's the first time I've said that to myself. The pain I'm in has been so bad that dying can only be a liberation. I don't want you to think that I've had a forlorn life. As I said, I am a single man and *yes*, I am here unaccompanied. But it's only because I haven't told anyone. How could I? After I'm gone I have letters awaiting postage that will explain to those I've left behind why I had to take such action. I can image my friends at the London club I frequent, or used to frequent, will have a drink in my honour. Ha! I just remembered I left a tab running. How slapdash and out of character of me, oh well.

There's no-one in particular who will miss me, I must admit. I was married once. I had a string of mistresses once. I'm sure the escort agency I used when I needed a woman for a social engagement, will miss my custom. The girl I saw last night in that hotel in London got the best tip I'd ever given anyone, including the waitress at the New York deli bar who found a business portfolio that I'd mislaid the preceding day. I think that was the only time in my thirty-five years in the industry that I broke into a sweat.

My 'legacy', as the solicitor called it, will be sold and all monies will go to a charitable trust – predictable, I know. I wanted to fund terrorism but it's so hard to know which terrorist group will give good value for money.

Leaving the department store, I have a short walk to the riverside apartment, the directions to which I've memorised, where I will spend my last hours. As I amble along the unfamiliar streets, the sun breaks through the snow filled clouds and its rays warm my face, sending a shiver all the way through me.

I've never thought about God before, but with the sun on my face the thought finally creeps up upon me. I considered myself to be a lay-agnostic. That is to say I have no understanding of the deep agnostical philosophy except the basic, 'we can't prove whether or not God exists'. I look at my watch. In just fourteen hours time I will know whether, well you know. Apparently God, if He does exist, doesn't like those who take their own lives, but if He does exist would he want one of His brood to be in pain? I'll put that to Him if I have to explain myself.

I never considered that I'd get cancer. I always thought it was something that happened to other people. When I was told that I had the illness, I did think 'why me?' But on the other hand I have led a very gratifying life, experienced so much and seen the world. I've done things that many will never do. If I hadn't been so well versed and travelled, I think I would have taken it worse. However, it did give me an excuse to finally take early retirement and go on a weeklong drinking session.

I walk beside the Limmet. The sun has departed, the Earth turning away from it, and it has begun to snow. My eyes are presented with yet more chocolate box images. The ducks on the river flap their wings and the street lights flicker on.

I'm at the apartment. I know my host will be waiting for me. I ring the bell. A sharp buzzing lets me. I pull open the glass-fronted door and enter the building. Apartment F is on the second floor. As I ascend the stairs I realise that I may not be walking out. I also wonder if the patrons of the apartment block know what goes on in apartment F. That sounds like a good title for a mystery novel. They must do I suppose. I knock on the white-painted door. Marina opens it and welcomes me in. We have spoken on the phone and via e-mail, but this is the first time we've met. Behind her stands Hans. He is the doctor who will leave me alone in the bedroom with a cocktail of barbiturates that I must knock back. I'll have ten minutes before I lose unconsciousness, then after fifteen minutes, I'll be dead.

Marina is short, mid-forties, with light blonde hair. We exchange pleasantries in German and she takes my bags. She introduces me to Hans. Hans looks like a doctor, well to me anyway. He's tall, with a sharp angular nose, black-rimmed glasses and a receding hairline. We shake hands, he welcomes me in English and I reply in German. Marina offers us a pot of coffee, which I happily accept. We sit at the kitchen table. The flat is exactly as the internet pictures showed. The front door opens directly into the kitchen, a short corridor leads to a bathroom and the two bedrooms, and a second door from the kitchen leads to the living room.

The apartment is sparsely decorated, minimalist. There's no clutter, few furnishings; the rooms that Marina shows me aren't blemished with any owner's personality. It's a blank, sanitary, canvas. I've reached heaven and I haven't even died yet.

After coffee and a sombre chat, Marina and Hans leave. Marina had offered to cook me dinner here in the flat tonight, but I'm not hungry, and besides, I couldn't bear the thought of my hygienic surroundings being raped by the heavy smell of cooked food, used utensils and dirty pans.

I pace the disinfected accommodation. In the corner of the second, smaller bedroom I find the miscellany of previous occupiers: a collection of walking sticks rest against a folded wheelchair.

I lean out of my bedroom window and see the city beyond, alive, lights glowing from all quarters. I'm happy to be here. Apparently James Joyce died in this country; I've found myself in good company.
I stay up most of the night. I can't sleep. I meander about the apartment, enjoying the magnificence of the sterilised rooms, immersing myself in the germ-free environment.

As dawn approaches I strip off, laying my suit, shirt and tie on the single bed. My underwear, vest and socks are folded up and placed in a spare polythene bag. In the bathroom I take pleasure in a stand-up wash with the new flannel and soap, and dry myself with the new towel. I place the now used soap, flannel and towel in the bag with my undergarments. I shave with the razor and foam, and after I've finished I also put them in the polythene bag, as I do with the moisturiser bottle, its contents smoothed across my body. After deodorising myself, I dress. I brush my hair and check my appearance in the bedroom mirror. I then pull open the clear packets that contain the toothbrush and toothpaste. After use they, along with the deodorant and comb, find themselves next the other items in the now full bag. The nail clippers and nail file lie with my wallet and passport in the bottom of my briefcase. I didn't need them after all. I give my shoes a rub down with the polish-cloth and it takes its place as my last used item.

The bedroom window is still open, letting in the wintry air. But it feels nice. I light a cigarette and contemplate the next few precious hours. I think about the predictable newspaper reports back home, the split columns in the newspaper as two academics or politicians argue their case for or against the catch-term 'euthanasia'; I think about the others I might inspire to take their lives into their own hands, so to speak.

Finishing the cigarette, I tie the clear plastic bag full of my used items and drop it to the ground. I do the same with my briefcase. I lift myself up on to the window ledge and drop. I put the polythene bag into the nearest bin. I have a plane to catch. I'm not really dying; my forged medical records, that I paid a premium for, help me get into these places. I get pleasure from the cleanliness of the apartments; I'm a bit obsessive compulsive, neurotic about grime and mess. I also get pleasure from the attention, the sincerity and seriousness of it all, it appeals to my dark sense of humour. I guess you could call me an 'assisted suicide tourist'. In fact you could dub me "Peter 'the euthanisaist' Wyreham". That fits. I'm off to Australia next, then on to Oregon and afterwards back to Holland. I can't wait.

*Note: The author recognises that the act portrayed in this work would be classed as 'physician assisted suicide'. However the title of the story remains due the character's obsession with the 'catch-term'.*

*(2006)*

**ladies and gentlemen, from Los Angles, California, the Doors!**

dark mystery
flames flicker
swirling
hypnotising
rush of organ
primal beats
psychedelic
six strings
rasped soul
vocals

late night
freeway
highway
eternity

visionary
dreams

we rest on
crystal rocks

setting sail on
oceans blue

the heart
breaks


*(2010)*

**the poets**

some have got
*it*
they write
crafting
effortless
verse
which flows
from pen
into lines
and rhythm
forming
structure
in front
of their
eyes

they have
a poetic
hammer

nailing
the words

the poem

every time


(2010)

**the streets awakens**

night fades to day
but dusty grey
clouds persist
holding back
first light

the rattle
and clang
of workers
rising to meet
another shift
by tube,
bus, bike, car,
and foot
comes to ear

finally a blue
sky succeeds
as the rumble of
traffic increases
and chatter breaks
the hush

I listen to the
dawn chorus
of a city


*(2010)*

**maudlin winter**

frozen dew
clings to blades of grass
beautiful crisp chill
stings flesh and throat

all opportunities seem far away
I live in a daydream

a hardy frost lingers
I contend with a cold vacant stare

remembering the torment
all that went before

the horror and terror
my vision precedes

lost friends
lost conversations
embracing dark nights

I fade beside an open fire

held breaths
the impudence of a candid remark
an unexpected shock
the sharp rays of morning sun

a rising wet fog
over a sweeping English vista
the winter sets in
I tender a farewell

(2009)

## check the amount and sign at the bottom

'check the amount and sign at the bottom,'
says the guy behind the till
I look him in his glazed eyes
one hand on the till
the other on the counter
he looks like he is thinking
about what he will do tonight
perhaps a few drinks with friends
or out with his girlfriend

I glance over at the girl to his left
I wished she'd served me
a beautiful woman
pale skin, fiery red hair
an autumnal dream
she's wearing a black low cut top
that leaves nothing to the imagination

I stare at the receipt
I can't even remember what I bought
it is all a blur under these hot lights
the temperature is unbearable
I think I'm going to collapse from exhaustion
I feel like Alex Guinness in Bridge Over The Kwai
standing out in the sun all day

all this in a spilt second
I look down
and with the black biro
the guy behind the till absently
handed to me wavering in my hand
I check the amount and sign at the bottom

*(2005)*

**strolling through London in the rain**

precipitation and dusk fall together
streetlights flicker on

vast glass shop windows emit light

and our arms wrapped around
each other dig further in

closer

soon puddles form on the pavement
and our feet splash through them all

I delight in the child-like joy
you have for everything
those innocent eyes
we should all have

back at the hotel
you manoeuvre
yourself to my side

resting your head on my shoulder

you whisper

*(2009)*

**coma nation**

everything is sterile
the air stifling
people
crazed
confused

apathy drinks in bars
dances in clubs
orders takeaways
fucks in bedsits
languishes in front
of the television

some try to make
a difference
but no one listens

nothing changes

*(2003)*

**no one knows who I am or what I do**


my mouth dries
when people
ask questions
*enquiring*
my eyes
flick from side to side
trying to find
an answer
in a lie
or a truth

and it's because
I know
deep down
they are
*you are*
not interested

I stay silent

smile, nod

everything
I am
everything
I do

a secret

and actually

I like it that way

*(2010)*

**england**

the indoor market
where my preconceptions
are blown away
the smell of raw meat and fish
lap together over the cut price
clothing, second-hand books,
knocked off homeware,
and grocery stalls

the aroma nauseating..... as it is intoxicating

a mecca for pensioners
those on a budget and the mentally ill
who wander in search
of paradise
the down-trodden faces
in 60's décor café
look up from their
red-top tabloids
their eggs and bacon
and take another
drag on their value cigarettes

depressing *but* real

I keep moving
on my way to the
dimly lit underground
Victorian toilets that reek
of over a hundred years
of urine and shit
thinking, 'hopes lies in the proles'

*(2004)*

**the sky exploded**

I sit in
dust
exposed
to the
elements
my limbs
seizing
my terrified
mind
watching
polished metal
turn to
rust

when the
sky
exploded

*(2008)*

## *The Supermarket Dissolved As The Past Echoed Through To The Present
### (with Heidi James)

*"Whatever our souls are made of, his and mine are the same."*
- Emily Bronte

I see myself - visible, present, and real in the grimy surface of the train window. Time has me in its grip, everyday, the office, meetings, lunches, dinners and a partner to find time to love. But I am giving it the slip, for what measure of time is there but memory and experience?

\*

The two-tone shades on the bathroom walls are fading like my memories. How did I end up here? Living in a rented house that is falling back into its composites. In a job that will see me to the grave, with no hope and a heavy heart, still craving and longing for a ghost from the past.

\*

Stopped at a station, families get on, get off. Someone is waiting on the platform, hands limp like rags, face brushed flat by the dirty light. A carrier bag floats like a spectre in the wind. The train convulses and pulls down the track again, slowly accumulating speed. The imposed geometry of the human landscape unfolds and reveals its gentle collapse under the dreadful weight of time, the train cutting through, keeping us in its speeding hollow, ageless and free.

\*

Looking into the bathroom mirror I barely recognise myself. My hair, once long, strong and plentiful, now short and receding like a battered Suffolk coastline. My skin tired, pitted, wrinkled and rough. But my

eyes still stare back at me with a hint of a sparkle that is now absent from the rest of me.
From a metal tap I run some lukewarm water into a pale blue basin. I coat my face in shaving foam and hesitate before bringing the blunt razor to my flesh.

\*

I remember us, and the sick triumphalism of our new love, holding hands and kissing in public. Lying on the grass in summer parks, drunk on cheap wine, his hand heavy on my young breast, his quick fingers teasing my expectant skin and the dark warmth of his mouth on my face. My love, he was mine. Much of who I am is because of him, because I was once his.

\*

Time has stripped, disjointed and unsettled thoughts that I once cherished. What I now have left is feelings. Feelings like the sun on our backs as we lay on the park, or the rich smell of Mexican food and the sweet smell of sugared pancakes drifting across a field full of thousands of people. Back then time stood still. The future was something we used to laugh about. But it catches up with you. The years have fallen away for me. I've spent so much time telling myself that something will happen, that I've stopped doing anything to make things happen.

\*

I saw the world through the false glow of his love for me. I have the tapes he made me of bands he thought I would and should like, flyers of gigs we went to, photos of him, the blue of his eyes reddened by the harsh flash; but I remember that blue and the black of his lashes, the red's and gold's in the captured in his hair and released by the sun. It is always summer in my memory of him. He is remembered as sensation – colour, taste and the drowsy smell of his baby-like skin.

\*

I dug through some boxes in the loft to find a shoebox that I had sealed many years ago, trapping the past and my torn feelings inside. Upon finding it, covered in dust and cobwebs, I just stared at it a while, almost afraid of what it contained. But I put my apprehensions aside and ripped away at brown tape that bound it. Inside, preserved for over a decade, lay pictures, hand written notes, which we used to leave for each other to find when we were apart, trinkets won from arcade games machines and Valentine, Birthday and Christmas cards. I lifted a card and opened it, she had written, 'I will always love you'. I closed my eyes, sighed and wondered what happened to that love?

*

I should have driven, but I need a drink. And time, time to find the girl he loved in the weathered woman I am now. I am so afraid of his disappointment. I'll talk too much, afraid of his silence, of him looking too deeply for too long. I wonder what he remembers of me. If I am part of the history he tells new acquaintances or if I am an absence in his new life. No-one touches me now the way he did then, we were each others first and most intense. My femininity was wonderful to him, the shallow curve of my hip, the cup of my bottom, the gentled drag of my breasts were incredible to his little boy hungers.

*

She was my first. I was aware, but in some ways, so unaware of sexuality. At first we just used to hold hands – her palms soft and reassuring in mine. Then we started kissing, our mouths complimenting the other, fitting like an uncomplicated jigsaw. As we grew together our kissing lasted longer and became deeper and our hands began to explore a body that wasn't ours. The excitement of my hands running along her soft curves, my eyes watching her breasts heave as she breathed. Alone in a bedroom, with parent's downstairs watching evening television and with younger siblings in a bedroom next door, we started to go further, the warmth of her vagina fresh of my fingers. She was leading me towards her heaven.

*

Now, the woman I am is tiring, I am old hat, boring and thickened about the waist by too many coupled dinners in an over-mortgaged dining room. Then, I was exciting, fresh. We would make love quietly in his bedroom at his mother's while she made us supper to eat in front of the telly, and fuck hard in toilets on trains, in bushes and alleyways behind the rows of houses near my school. I sucked the tender head of his cock while kneeling under a table at MacDonald's, his burger forgotten on the plastic tabletop. I delighted in him and the alien solidity of his male body.

*

I dress in newly purchased clothes to cover a body that has surrendered itself to age. I spent money that should have been used on loan repayments for the new threads. For the hour we will spend together I want her to see me looking as well as I think I now can. I want to impress her. But new clothes can't hide the story that is written across my face. How I yearn now to be young and carefree once again. To be in love, embracing each new dawn. On a summer's day, like today, years ago, we'd go to the heath and she'd take me in hand between the overgrown gorse and ferns.

*

My stomach blistered when I turned from the dull contours of tins of soup and beans in the supermarket straight into the placid beauty of his face. Thank God I was alone, and with lipstick still fresh from work. I pretended to be in a hurry, couldn't speak, couldn't compose myself around his presence so shoved a business card at him, I wonder now if I wanted to impress him with my business title, but then I just wanted to get away and calm down.

*

I found myself absently walking the warm aisles of the supermarket after I'd seen her, my eyes absorbing the colours as my mind pictured us all those years ago. She still looked the same. The confident walk, the kind face, the rich dark hair, the slender figure, its all there; she's just slightly older; time has added a distinguished brush to her. She's become the woman I always thought she would become strong, independent and full of life. Her voice was light, her eyes welcoming, but only inviting me so far; did she give me her business card as a full stop to end an unwelcome awkward moment? Will I become just a note in her diary? As I walked the aisles I imagined her life now, her family - a strong masculine husband, his features cut from stone, her children healthily, intelligent, well behaved with good Christian names.

*

And he phoned. He phoned me at work, his voice solidified in the network. I am lost. I am spinning a new future with him, I am leaving my life and moving back with him and the girl I was. We are having children and dogs and a garden that we dig. We are making love in our own bed and listening to the moth like breathes of our babies. I am stroking his hair as he sleeps. Yet when we meet, it will be a drink, a deceitful lunch and a vacancy where once we talked non-stop. He will have a beautiful girlfriend, a wife, and children already perfect. He is just curious, I am longing.

*

In my badly decorated front room I sat perched on the edge of a sofa that has seen better days. The curtains were closed letting through a dull light, as outside the rain fell. It took me several tries at calling. I'd dial the number but disconnect before it rang, my nervous getting the better of me. I felt like a teenager, full of butterflies and self-doubt. Finally, I let it ring and she answered with an expectant tone. Our conversation was once again brief, stilted, punctuated with pregnant pauses, but there was something, something about that way our voices met along the telephone wire.

*

I could stay on the train; I could go back and never expose myself to this. What am I doing opening myself up to humiliation, to his scathing view, I should leave him with his vision of me when I left him, finally, to go to University. Would he care? Is he even there, is he coming or is he too backing out, picturing the tired me that confronted him at the shop? I stay, too scared to move too brave to run home. I'll meet him, and kiss him just once more. Then the adult realities will seep in and maybe I'll even realise I am better off where I am, comfortable and plump. I thought love would last forever, that love was divine – unrestrained by time, unseen like God, but now I know I was wrong.

*

I find myself in film, moving slowly in sepia. The city and the people walking alongside and towards me fade. Will she be there? Or am I still living the dream of her returning to me after all these years? My stomach ties itself in knots as I open the restaurant door and go in.

*(2005)*

**the jam**

cars
in line
break lights
red
a sea
of frustration
matrix
signs
taunting
wheels turn
moving only
a few metres

across the carriage
way
they fly

headlights
a flare

we wait
overheating
like our
engines


*(2010)*

**contorted with passion**

looking down into the
chipped, white plastic coated
metal basket that had an
A4 poster stuck on it
with one word printed: reduced

my eyes rested upon a cd cover

four guys leading an attack on stage
the singer falling into his mike
his face contorted with passion
the guitarist and bassist
throwing poses as the
drummer sweated out a rhythm

I recognised the name of the group

they called the album, 'the story of…'
it was a compilation, the best tunes

I had to have it

i picked it up and it d i s a p p e a r e d
into my jacket pocket

I walked out of the shop

I've always thought the guys in
*the Clash* would have approved

(2007)

**I don't want to lose you before love has begun**


we stroll
hand in hand
under an autumn night's
sky; stars present, crisp chill
walking into a dimly
lit pub; oak beams, chipped plaster walls
adorned with relics of a bygone age,
there's space by the
fire; logs slowly burning,
we sit
sip our drinks
our fourth metacarpals touch
they dance
we smile
we've talked so much
but you still hold back
I want to embrace you
but stop,
hesitant,
because I don't want to
lose you before love has
begun


(2009)

**unannounced**

in the distance
cargo ships,
lights illuminated,
as the night and
mysterious dark clouds
roll in on a stiff wind

the sea crashes into
the coastal defences,
an untameable
force of nature

then, the moon,
unannounced,
cuts through the clouds,
sun reflected on its surface

that radiance cast down
onto crystal clear
shimmering water

*(2010)*

# Cadence

It comes down in sheets the warm southern rain. I stand on a dark wooden veranda, in front of a tobacconist's store, smoking a cigarette from a newly bought pack of Chesterfield Kings watching people rush about their business. New Orleans glistens beneath the shower in the humid late afternoon. During unexpected break in traffic; mopeds and rusty cars, silence descends and somewhere above, "hm-a-hur-hm-ahur- hm-a-hur-hm-ahur" emanates from one of the overhanging apartments; a melody hummed in a deep feminine bluesy pitch.

The stench of tobacco drapes itself around the tavern. In the corner on an uneven stage, an old Pearl kit is set up. The bass drum must be as old as building, its circumference wide, the pedal, part wood and metal. I've found myself pushed back against many a brick wall in tiny pubs and clubs, no room to move, sweat pouring, stinging my eyes, my arms turning to jelly as I kept the beat going.

My first kit, bought for my fourteenth birthday, was a black Yamaha five piece and came from a second hand music store. It had scratches and dents; the cymbals chipped. But, like a first romance, the kit was my first love. I would polish it, happy when I could see my reflection in the black plastic trim on the toms and bass drum. But now, fifteen years later, I only have the high-hat stand left from that original set.

I return to the hotel that I'm staying in. I go up to my room and drop my damp coat on the wooden floor and lie down on the bed. The wallpaper, a faded and stained dirty yellow, is peeling from the walls, pulling thin plaster away from brick. Lying back on the bed I watch flies dodge the blades of the ceiling fan. Rhythms enter my mind and I start humming a Skin Yard song. This leads me on to contemplating who is the best drummer to come out of the Seattle grunge scene of the nineteen nineties. I've been in town for two weeks now, but previous to that I'd fulfilled a teenage dream by visiting the Emerald City, a place I'd long been enamoured having given me the soundtrack to my adolescent years; Malfunkshun, Green River, Mother Love Bone….

Drummers though, my top candidates: Barrett Martin, Matt Cameron, Matt Chamberlain and Dave Grohl. Dave certainly had the power, Barrett good fills, done some great work with Screaming Trees. Chamberlain, maybe a bit light, but solid enough, Matt Cameron highly versatile, a real workhorse live, although maybe a bit busy a times.

The first band I was in, after two school covers bands, was heavy influenced by grunge with, it has to be said, an added touch of Metallica-esque heavy metal. We were a three piece, P on guitar/vocals, myself on drums, with a revolving door policy on bassists. We were collectively known as Grass, an asinine moniker, but we thought it was okay at the time. We saved what little money we earned in various post-school dead end jobs on improving on what little equipment we had. The band lasted around three years and we had some really good tunes, very punk, very heavy, we had quite a following. In that time I think we must have played every pub in East Anglia that would put a band on. We split when P, who couldn't get through his day without dropping several E's and smoking weed continually, stopped turning up for rehearsals and then gigs. We had recorded a demo with Matt Johnson producing. Roadrunner Records were interested but P was more attracted to staying up all night, getting stoned, whilst listening to techno and waiting for the sun to come up. So that was the finish of that.

The rain has stopped. The air that had been cooled by the precipitation now, once again, turns muggy. I get up from the bed, unbutton my shirt and throw it on to the bed, I turn on the radio and tune into the local radio station. I pick up my Vic Firth drumsticks and start tapping on the snare drum I have set up in the room. I'm looking forward to tonight. As soon as I got in town, two weeks ago, I immediately started looking for some guys to jam with. I found adverts and approached some buskers in the street. It wasn't long before I was working a second hand kit, borrowed from Max's Music, in a disused and damaged garage, left vacant after hurricane Katrina brought her devastation, the four of us, me the solitary whitey, making magic music in the heart of desolation, a mixture of jazz, blues, bluegrass and soul.

After the disintegration of Grass I didn't play for a year. I got a job in a record shop, spent more time going out to bars and clubs, having fun, enjoying life. But I always felt that something was missing, bring music back into my life was something I need to do. But I knew I didn't just want to play generic rock music and I didn't just want to be another drummer. I wanted to be the best, or as pre-eminent as I could; I sought to become skilled at as many styles as possible.

I had never had any lessons, well I had a dozen when I initially started; it was an unfulfilling experience. The tutor would leave me in tapping on the kit whilst he looked after his children in another room.

I learnt by putting on headphones and listening to tunes with the volume turned up high, just playing along. I would practice every spare moment of the day. I was fortunate enough that parents didn't use their garage so I was able to sound proof it with empty egg boxes and thus make as much noise as I could. In summer it got so hot in there, perspiration would run from ever pore. I also needed to build strength up in my arms so I had a punch bag hanging in the garage and would go ten rounds with it everyday.

*(2008)*

**stallone**

late night
beers drunk
fire burning
watching
an old
stallone movie
dude has
the physique of
a Greek God
the pathos
of a Greek philosopher
and when backed
into a corner
he comes
out fighting
like a Greek warrior


*(2010)*

**sanctuary in a magritte**


a small victory
as all I seem to do is sleep
take a long drive
time moves as it pleases

sanctuary in a magritte
solitude is a fact
in life and in love

no longevity in mortality
or life in vitality
currently learning
that I'm not a god

the postcards you sent me
remind me that your not here

in the sky and in the heart


*(1998)*

**sympathetic, but swift**

she blew out
the candle I lit
for her
sympathetic,
but swift

now she's
being romanced
talking like
her and him
are the first
lovers the
world has ever
known
or have
ascended
to a plain
that's hasn't been
touched
since
burton and taylor

I wait for it
to end
lit match hovering
over wick and wax

fingers getting
burnt

*(2010)*

**new york (an announcement)**


calling all stations
wake up to a new beat!
the city is on fire
and has been for weeks!

they said it wouldn't happen
but just look at us now
I made one million dollars
and spent it all down town

the suits have the loot
it's in their briefcases
that they hold the real power
whilst the poor look up
they look down
and it's in their wealth
that they're likely to drown

as the city heat bakes the feet
of one million soles (souls)
insurance costs will cover the cost
of the fire in park hill

executive lunches in the hot midday sun
the homeless search for a single coin to bum

the smell of sweat pollutes the air
just as the smog does

but I'm in my company car
stuck in my tenth traffic jam
the roads are veins and the heart almost stops


(1996)

**your secrets**

at night, it's beautiful
there's a shore
soft sand and pebbles
the moon reflects
off the breaking waves
and you, your smile, shines
opening heaven
in my heart
in the sky
I ask you for your secrets
you play with your hair
and ask me 'what next?'
we dance to a soundtrack
that plays in our souls
it's lilting and uplifting
melancholic and haunting
it's elegant, like you,
and we're astray
caught in each other's gaze
your blue eyes, mine grey
our smiles ache
your hands grip mine
the waves collapse
a chill breeze grasps
we cling, embrace,
i memorise the rhythm of your
heart beats
you place my hand
on your belly and whisper
we kiss, I drown in
your love, I ask you for
your secrets

*(2009)*

**and she knows it**

she sits opposite

but I'm aware that

I ain't got much to offer
this nordic goddess
this scandinavian angel
this bergen beauty

her good looks
her magnificent
long blonde hair
her blue eyes
her soft skin
her cultured mind

deserve more than

cheap nights out
cheap hotel rooms
and cheap words
recycled from bad movies
coupled with my
unconvincing lies

I ain't got much to offer

and
she
knows
it

*(2010)*

**the comeback**

back in the ring

dusting off
pen and paper
brushing down
rhythm and words

sizing up
stanzas and couplets
firing off
metre and lines

ducking and diving

full contact blows

each punch
each hit
landing
counting
ensuring

I avoid
the
blank
cold canvas

looking for a
knockout

with
words

*(2008)*

# The Writer

He felt like he could neither justify nor condemn his actions; he acted, he said, with emotion and felt that his emotions were above scrutiny.

We changed the subject momentarily and talked about his book(s).

"It's an epic good versus evil story set in 1920s Chicago," he told me, speaking as if it were already a best seller - but then again a writer should have faith in his work.
"Sounds interesting."
"Well, I've nearly finished it. Five re-writes and a change in setting, but I've kept the title the same, The Light Corridor."
"I've always liked the title. I'd be interested in reading it. What about the other two?"
"My other two books?
"Yeah, have you finished those?"
"Well, Mascot is half way there and The Bear and The Fox needs some editing."
"What about Going Nowhere? Are you going to send that off again?"
"I looked at it the other day, it's a good story, but I've changed in terms of style, so I might rewrite it."
"Why don't you concentrate on one novel? At least get one finished?"
"I would, but I'll be writing The Bear and The Fox and then I'll get fed up with the contemporary setting and need to write some fantasy."
"Right. So what are you going to do about Serena?"
"I guess I'll phone her."
"Is that a good idea?"
"A man needs to sow his seed."
"I thought she'd gone a bit, you know?"
"Yeah, she is a bit off the wall, but when I have that arse in my hand…"
"I understand."
He turned and went into the kitchen and I changed channels on the television.

(2004)

**golden tanned flesh**

emerging from
the sea
droplets of
water, just
beads, unbroken,
roll, trickle
down your
golden tanned flesh
you return to me
and we
bathe under
a cloudless blue sky
and a radiant sun

*(2009)*

**feel all famous five**

out here
I'm free

the fields,
some ploughed,
some with crops golden
stretch beyond for miles
forests deep and wide
impenetrable
full of mystery

I feel all famous five
bicycling away from the world
off road, on road

adventure, exercise

fresh air
stings my lungs

I marvel at nature
its beauty
which never fails
to enlighten
to inspire

and I know how fortunate I am
to have been able to stop
and look around

i've been loved
and I've loved

(2010)

## 2012 Second Edition Bonus Content

## baby, there's an app for that

you tease me with your twittering
and your ciphered posts on your blog
I follow you around the Internet
to the forums on which you log

your candid status updates
let me glimpse into your affections
I want to get connected
but why won't you make a connection?

I know you receive my emails
because I receive a read receipt
this waiting is driving me to distraction
I can't drink, sleep or eat

I've lost count of the hours
I've loitered for you on skype
in the past if you were away from your computer
and the cherry keyboard on which you type
you'd reply via your blackberry, but now
it's all about your apple, on orange, i-phone
how many fruits will you go through?
honey, in this multimedia world I feel so alone

when I log on to MSN it says that you're offline
but I really think you're there
smiling at your elusivity, whilst I linger
make up words and give a hopeful stare

I open up another tab and Google your name
it's not about your Facebook, Flickr, Myspace or Bebo
your LinkedIn profile doesn't tell me

anything that I don't all ready know

I want to poke you to let you know I'm near
but my Internet can't cope and rejection is a fear

tv programmes 24/7 on command
sweetheart, why can't you be on demand?

and when I finally receive a text, you tell me:
'it's been hectic' and 'it's hard to stay on track'
I scroll through my new purchase
and reply: 'baby, there's an app for that'


*(2010)*

## November Hotel

"Let me have a drag on that bad motherfucker," J asked.

P passed 'The Killer' over. 'The Killer' was part menthol tobacco, part cigar, and part weed. Many a man had been floored by a drag on that beast. J took a hit like he was breathing in fresh mountain air and washed it down with a shot of JD.

"Did you hear about the Monkey?"

"No?" P replied.

"He's doing bird."

"How come?"

"Well." J he took another drag. "One day he woke and thought he was Jesus Christ."

P raised an eyebrow. "Oh?"

"He went down to the *clinic*, you know the one where you go to get checked out for sexual diseases. Started bothering the woman, you know, saying he was Christ and that he could cure them by placing his hand on their parts."

"Crazy...."

"Yeah, well one woman had the clap real bad. The Monkey got lucky. Got his hand down there."

"Shit...."

"The next thing that happened the mother of this woman grabs him, and you know The Monkey's a skinny guy, throws him to the ground and calls the police. Turns out that wasn't the first stunt he'd pulled around town. Remember hearing about that guy who used to sit around in the swimming pools, looking at the women, dressed as a Sheik?"

"The one who had the video camera?"

"Yeah. That was The Monkey."

"Son-of-a...."

"Anyway he's doing porridge now. I heard his arsehole is as big as a clowns pocket."

P cackled. "Sick bastard properly enjoys it."

"I don't know." J continued puffing on The Killer. "Apparently there's a guy in there with a ten by four inch dick. They call him Horse."

"Shit."

"Don't know if any woman or man could take that length. Anyway, I need to take a slash. Then I'll get a round in. Whatcha havin? Same again?"

"Yeah, but make it straight."

"Okay."

J crossed the floor taking in the stare from the brunette behind the bar. He pushed open the door to the can and walked in. Dropping the butt of The Killer into the urinal, he undone the zip on his trousers, took out his tool and pissed out the beer and JD he'd been drinking for the last three or so hours.

\*

"…so what did he say?"

"He said he was a lawyer."

"A lawyer?"

"Yeah, he looked like one you know. Dressed up to the nines, suited and booted, flashing the cash."

"Great."

"Well, it wasn't."

"So what happened again?"

"Well, we're talking, you know, getting on really well, tells me all about himself. Says he really likes blondes. He's really eyeing me…."

"You weren't wearing *that* dress were you?"

"Yeah, of course! Anyway, I tell him about myself, the family, I start telling him about Dad being the owner of the November Hotels chain…."

"Oh, I bet that kept him interested."

"Well, that's when he started to get weird you know? He got up saying that he was going to the toilet, but he went over to speak to these two men who were standing by the bar. Anyway, he came back and started asking me all these strange questions about Dad."

"So you got up and left?"

"Well, no, I liked him, besides he did stop. He started to ask about me, I told him about my college course. He brought some more drinks, we started kissing, but then he started to get pushy, touching me up."

"Did you tell he to get off? Didn't the bouncers help?"

"One looked over but walked away as if they were to scared to do anything."

"So then what happened?"

"Well, he tried to put his hand up my dress, saying that he was going to fuck me."

"Oh my God...."

"Well, that's when that bloke they found in the river came over and pulled me away. The lawyer guy went fucking mental started smashing the place up, so I ran."

"Sounds frightening."

"Yeah, anyway, I'd better make a move."

"What time do you have to be at college?"

"Eight o'clock. I'm here now sitting in the car"

"Oh, right. What time will you be round?"

"Well, I'll be finished here at nine, so half nine?"

"Ok, see you then, bye."

"Bye."

*

J approached the bar. "Hey, Marie."

"Hi, same again?"

"Yeah, but make it straight for P."

"Ok." Marie started to get the drinks together. "Did you hear about The Monkey?"

"Yeah."

"Dirty bastard. You know I made it with him?"

"Really?"

"Yeah, it was small and went off really quick. I thought he was such a sweet guy, he told me my eyes were as blue as the sea, such a poet."

J watched Marie's breasts now there was poetry, he thought.

Marie came back with the drinks. "That will be £3.90."

"Thanks." J passed over a five note. "Oh and Marie...."

"Yeah?"

"My love for you grows everyday, I want to take you now, but I don't know what to say."

Marie laughed and walked to the till.

J stared at her arse.

"Here you go." She passed him his change and her phone number.

J smiled and took the drinks back to P.

P was smoking a Marlboro Red. J passed him his drink and P passed J a smoke. "Cheers."

"Cheers." P took a mouthful of scotch. "We'd better drink up. *The call has just come through.*"

J nodded his head and sank his JD in one. "Okay bro, let's go."

They got up and left.

Out in the cold night air, J and P lit up another smoke and started the short walk to their vehicle.

"Have you heard the one about the man and his wife who go to bed on their wedding anniversary?" J took a pull on his smoke.

"No."

"Well, it's the night of their wedding anniversary and he whispers to her, 'Can we try something kinky tonight?' She turns to look at him and asks, 'What do you have in mind?' He says 'Can I put my length in your ear?'"

"Ha ha ha."

"She replies, 'But it might make me go deaf!' Her husband says, 'Well I've been coming in your mouth for the last 20 years and it hasn't stopped you talking!'"

"Ha ha ha." P blew out the last hit on his smoke. "That's fucking, good man." He threw the smoke to the floor. "Fucking good." P unlocked the doors to the black BM and they both got in.

"Where is the pick up?" J lit up another smoke.

"Not far. Not far."

The black BMW pulled up in the car park of a community college.

"What does she look like again?"

"Here." P passed a photo over to J.

"Ha." J laughed and shook his head. "They're always blondes."

"Yeah, ain't that true."

"Okay, you ask the question, I'll open the door."

"Cool."

The small hand of the clock on the dash of the car hit nine. A few minutes passed and the students from the college began to file out of the building.

"Okay. Nice and slow."

P started the engine and they waited for the blonde. "There she is."

They watched as the blonde walked down the college steps and bid goodbye to her fellow pupils. She turned and began to walk towards a dimly lit car park.

J got out of the car, pulled on a pair of black leather gloves and started to walk. P drove off ahead of him and slowly pulled up along side the blonde. The electric window on the passenger's side came down and P lent across.

"Excuse me."

The blonde looked over and bent down. "Yes."

"Do you know where the train station is?"

"Err, yeah." The blonde hesitated. "If you...."

J rushed up and took out of his pocket a handkerchief that he had just soaked in chloroform. He wrapped his arm around the blonde's neck. She began to struggle and attempted a scream. J covered her mouth with the soaked cloth. Her fighting body went limp. J pulled her around to the back seat door; he opened the door and pushed the blonde inside, then got in himself. P hit the accelerator and pulled off.

P passed J a Marlboro Red. They both lit up.

"Lets have some tunes to pass the time."

"Okay." P reached down and slipped a CD into the player. "You like Dexter Gordon?"

"Yeah, man."

P hit play.

Smooth jazz echoed around the car.

J took a drag on the smoke. "Have you heard the one about the two goldfish?"

*(2004)*

**after….**

I wipe my brow
my vision refocuses

it's over

that built-up passion
which felt like it could
have powered a nation

gone

I pass her
some cheap
white tissue
for her to wipe
herself up with

after the act
my girl
wants to hug
and kiss
lie in the
after glow
of our love

but
I want to either
down a few more beers
or roll over
and go to sleep


(2000)

## schoolgirls look more like porn stars these days

I worked for a while
in a convenience store
near a high school
everyday they'd come in
aged around 14-16 years
painted faces, short skirts, high heels

and then on the weekends
as I drank and smoked
in my favourite night spot
I'd see the same girls
illegally enjoy the night
hanging together in
a tight group
shy and apprehensive
in such an adult environment
painted up and wearing
shorter skirts, higher heels
their slender frames
silhouetted by the various
coloured lights sweeping
the dance floor

the guys would move in
picking off the girls
in the group one by one

their loss of innocence
sealed in a car park
or a back seat
or knees grazed
on broken concrete

*(2003)*

**the girl with the jet black hair**

our fucks
    primal
sucking
thrusting
bites
sweat

the
screaming
beats
of our
hearts

just inches
away
from touching

i want you
to drown

in my
cum

but it
swims
in
your
belly

we listen

(2005)

**the last dance**

there was something about her
defined and dignified

I knocked my shot back
and dropped the glass on the bar

I watched as she danced to
'it ain't over till it's over' by lenny kravitz

the couples on the dance floor parted
and the men watched on
as she rocked gently to the groove

my eyes transfixed
as she swayed her hips
flinging her hair
from side to side
her arms raised
grinding

I approached
she looked up
our eyes met
we smiled

she was wearing a tee
which read: 'tonight, i'm single'

at least we'd have
something in common I thought

*(2004)*

**an immortal line**


it came to me when inspiration
always seems come

just as I'm falling to sleep
drifting into a dream
lying in a warm bed
next to a warm body
after a hard day
doing what ever I do

it was good, a great line
an immortal line
I line that I would fight all day for

but I was unwilling to get up
and write it down

would I remember it in the morning?

the line went over and over in my mind
damn it was good, I'd remember it
yeah, I'd remember it, no….

l had to write it down
I pulled myself up from the warmth
from my slumber to find a pen
a scrap of paper, to scratch it down

I returned to bed, returned to the heat
and closed my eyes
praying that the next line didn't come


*(2003)*

**and I snapped**

I overturned the table
we were sat at
threw a chair in the air
started screaming obscenities
labelling my girl
a whore, a bitch
every foul word
I could think of

I kicked the cat
and thought about
strangling my girl

instead I left the room
slamming the door behind me

I went and lay on the bed
and cried

she had done nothing wrong
simply asking me questions
about my day

I can't bear to think
about how I spend my time
isolated, caged
too afraid to go outside
I hate being questioned
about anything

I want to be on my own
but solitude makes demons of us all

*(2003)*

**elsewhere**

finishing off
in my girl's
best friend's
curly brown
pubic hairs
she's not on
the pill
and I didn't have
a rubber

the ecstasy of
the moment is
always overshadowed
by a slight feeling
of guilt

we relax back
on her futon
and I recall a summer
when all I did was
play football and
drink lemonade

*(2002)*

James D Quinton lives in the UK

Also by the same author

Fiction

Touch
The Victorian Time Traveller

Poetry

Street Psalms
The City Is On Fire And Has Been For Weeks

www.ingramcontent.com/pod-product-compliance
Lightning Source LLC
Chambersburg PA
CBHW032019040426
42448CB00006B/670